Milan in 3 Days:

The Definitive Tourist Guide Book That Helps You Travel
Smart and Save Time

Book Description

It seems like there is too little time today to visit all the places you'd like to see. But even if you only have three days, you can get to know Milan. But don't waste that precious time wandering around looking around for the best sights and restaurants, to decide what you really want to see.

That's why we have developed the **Travel Smart & Save Time Guides.** We do the research for you. We put together the best choices in the area, so that you can select the hotel, restaurants and attractions you want to include in your stay. We simply help you like no other travel guide can.

Milan has architectural treasures, markets, museums and many other attractions that draw tourists from around the world. We'll make sure you have time to hit the ones most important to most travelers.

We offer three-day vacation plans with top-rated hotels in three price ranges, restaurants with all types of food and various price points, and descriptions of all the sights you won't want to miss. You'll learn:

- How to get to Milan by air

- Getting from the airport into the city

- How to get around by metro, bus or tram

- The top luxury, mid-range and budget hotels in Milan

- Where you'll want to eat, to hit all the favorite cuisines of the area

- What you can't miss visiting, as well as a few off-the-beaten-path choices

- Where to celebrate the night away, if you're into hot music and dancing

We will save you time and money, and stress, too! This travel guide helps you to enjoy the best vacation days you'll spend in Milan.

The People of Milan

Some travelers feel that the people of Milan seem to be rude, but that's simply not true. People in Milan rarely will make the first step to create or maintain contact with others. They have their own circle of people that they are comfortable with, and that's where their interest lays.

Milanese people are focused on career and job prospects. They want to make more money (don't we all?). They travel to the beaches of Liguria on summer weekends and head for the Alps for winter vacations. There are not many locals on the streets on weekends.

People in Milan are careful what they look like, but are not prone to driving extremely flashy cars unless they are football (read: "soccer") players or famous people in their circle of friends.

Language

The central dialect of Lombard that is spoken in Milan is known as Milanese. Since Milan is an important Italian city, this dialect is important in business dealings.

Milanese is quite often considered an Italian dialect, but it's actually more a Western Romance language. It is related to Romansh, French and other languages that are referred to as Gallo-Italian.

Holidays

Jan 1	New Year's Day	National holiday
March	March Equinox	Season
April	Good Friday	Observance
April	Easter Day	National holiday
April	Easter Monday	National holiday
Apr 25	Liberation Day	National holiday
May 1	Labor Day / May Day	National holiday

June 2	Republic Day	National holiday
June	June Solstice	Season
Sept 22	September Equinox	Season
Nov 1	All Saints' Day	National holiday
Dec 7	The Feast of St. Ambrose	Local Milan holiday
Dec 8	Feast of the Immaculate Conception National holiday	
December	December Solstice	Season
Dec 25	Christmas Day	National holiday
Dec 26	St. Stephen's Day	National holiday
Dec 31	New Year's Eve	Observance

Religious Beliefs

As is most of Italy, the population of Milan is mainly Catholic. Over 95% of the Milanese population described themselves as Roman Catholic in 2004.

Other religions practiced there include Protestantism, Judaism and Islam.

Here is a quick preview of what you will learn in this tourist guide:

- Helpful information about Milan

- Flying into the city

- Transportation tips in town

- Why Milan is such a vibrant tourist spot and what you will find most remarkable about it

- Information on luxury and budget accommodations

- The currency used in Milan

- Tourist attractions you should make time to see

- Other attractions for entertainment and culture

- Events that may be running during your stay

- Tips on the best places to eat & drink for all price points, whether you want simple fare, worldwide dishes or Italian flavor

Table of Contents

1. Introduction 10

2. Key Information about Milan.................................17

3. Transport to and in Milan 20

4. Accommodations 27

5. Sightseeing... 37

6. Eat & Drink...41

7. Culture and Entertainment 47

8. Special Events in Milan..52

9. Safety in Milan...55

10. Conclusion 57

1. Introduction

Milan is the main financial center of Italy. The population is second only to Rome, but Milan is the center of the largest metropolitan and urban area in the country.

People who have never visited Milan do not consider it to be as beautiful as other cities in Italy. It was partially destroyed in bombing raids in WW II. However, the residents have rebuilt the city as a thriving business capital.

What makes Milan interesting to so many people is its lifestyle. There is great interest in opera, shopping, nightlife and football ("soccer"). It is also the center for the Italian fashion industry. Two times each year, paparazzi, fashion aficionados and supermodels declare the city their own for the spring and fall fashion fairs. Although Milan has modern aspects, it is still among the most ancient of European cities, and its architecture reflects this.

Milan is most famous for its historical sights, including La Scala, a historic opera house; the Duomo, a large and grand Gothic cathedral; the Pirelli Tower, a wonderful example of modernistic 1960's Italian architecture; the Brera Art Gallery, with among the finest of European artistic works; the Galleria Vittorio Emanuele, a glamorous and ancient shopping gallery; and Santa Maria alle Grazie Basilica, which houses Leonardo da Vinci's famous painting The Last Supper.

A Brief History of Milan

Milan was founded by Celtic peoples in the 7th century BC. By 222 BC, Romans occupied the city and it was called Mediolanum. The city became a vital commerce point because it holds a strategic position on trade routes leading from Rome to the rest of Europe.

Milan experienced a peaceful period, but it was shattered by invasions of barbarians. The town council (COMUNI) began to grow, however, in the 1000's AD, through 1162. In that year, the Holy Roman Emperor, Federico Barbarossa, attacked the town, using local conflicts for his own advantage. However, the town rose up against him, and in 1176, the Lega Lombarda dispersed the invaders.

From the 1200s on, the Torrianis, Viscontis and Sforza would govern the city. Milan became more powerful during this time. Spanish rule fell over Milan in 1535, and then it was given to the country of Austria in 1713. Milan became the capital of the Italian republic in 1802.

After Austria dominated the city from 1814 to 1859, Napoleon III and Vittorio Emanuele II dismissed the Austrians. Milan became part of the Italian Kingdom in 1860.

Neighborhoods

Navigli

A metro ride or walk through Milan will lead you to this district, known for its bars, restaurants and cafes that stand side by side on the streets that line its quaint canals. People-watching is a prime pastime in this area. The neighborhood after dark is buzzing, with well-known hotspots for Milan nightlife.

Navigli also hosts antiques markets the last Sunday of every month. Treasures spread all the way out to the da Vinci-designed Naviglio Grande Canal. The neighborhood is a mecca for treasure hunters and photographers. You can wander the many stalls and check out things like jewelry, books, furs, old records and antique furniture. When your legs are tired, there are lots of places where you can relax with a drink or a bite to eat.

Brera

Situated just north of the Duomo and often called artsy and bohemian, this neighborhood is home to restaurants, shops and galleries. It's a great place to wander. It feels like a smaller city, with its narrow alleys and streets.

Piazza Duomo

Here, tourists often visit the inside of the famous Cathedral of Santa Maria Nascente and marvel at the exterior, as well. The elevator or steps take you to a rooftop viewing terrace.

In addition, La Rinascente department store has a top floor that is a foodie paradise. The small restaurants and gourmet foods are worth the trip up. The seventh floor also has a terrace with a great view. It is quite possibly the best view of Il Duomo (the cathedral). It looks almost close enough to touch!

Porta Garibaldi

This is a wonderful place for walking, eating and watching people. There are shops and cafes, and the wonderful art in 10 Corso Como. It may be difficult to select the restaurant you prefer from all the cafes and restaurants that line Corso Como and Corso Garibaldi.

What does Milan offer its Visitors?

If you're visiting Milan for the first time, the Cathedral Duomo di Milano is a masterpiece of Gothic architecture that must be experienced to be believed. It will take your breath away, and it's the most iconic attraction of Milan.

In front of Il Duomo, the piazza holds court like Milan's reception hall. It's quite busy, with many people meeting there, before heading off to the cafes and shops that skirt the area.

After you have seen the "main attractions" and marveled at the architecture, explore a bit deeper and discover beautiful spots and Milanese history. There are also plentiful shopping, art and nightlife possibilities in Milan.

2. Key Information about Milan

Money Matters

Italy is a member country of the European Union and uses the euro as its currency. The euro is sub-divided into 100 euro cents.

Notes are issued in denominations of €5, €10, €20, €50, €100, €200 and €500. Each note has a color all its own.

Coins are issued in 1 cent, 2 cents, 5 cents, 10 cents, 20 cents, 50 cents, €1 and €2 denominations.

As you arrive in Milan, exchange your traveler's checks or currency at a local bank, rather than an exchange bureau, shop or hotel, since those have higher commissions and rates. In addition, most of the local hotels accept major branded credit and debit cards.

ATMs

It's easy to get cash from ATMs in Milan. Visa and Mastercard both have global credit card networks. Note that your fees may be higher when you use your card at foreign ATMs.

Credit Cards

This is the safest way for you to carry money. They have fairly good exchange rates and you can use them for cash advances.

Tipping

In most instances, you will not be expected to tip in Milan. But of you have received great service, meeting or exceeding your standards, you may feel free to tip.

Restaurant Tipping

Service charges are sometimes added to restaurant bills. They range from 10 to 15%. Some even add charges for bread, plates, tablecloth and silverware!

This is actually normal, but check the bill before you tip.

If there are no service charges on your bill, tourists usually round the bill up, like leaving 20 Euros for a bill of 18 Euros for a meal.

Hotel Tipping

You aren't required to tip at Milan hotels, but the staff does appreciate it. The porter or bellboy is usually tipped up to 5 Euros, but rarely more. If the concierge helps you in some way, you can leave a couple of Euros. The housekeeper will appreciate .75 to 1.50 Euro for each day of your stay. For room service and valets, a .50 Euro gratuity is sufficient.

3. Transport to and in Milan

Getting to Milan by Plane

Malpensa Airport is the largest Milanese international airport that serves the metro Milan area of northern Italy. The airport is about 30 miles from the center of Milan. They have two runways and two terminals for passengers, and a separate cargo terminal.

Malpensa Airport handled more than 19 million passengers in 2016. It is the second most used Italian airport for international passengers.

Getting to Milan from the Airport

Bus

Malpensa Bus Express and Malpensa Shuttle connect the airport to the central station in Milan. The shuttle bus stops at both terminals 1 & 2 and at

Milan Fair and Busto Arsizio, if someone requests it. The trip takes between 60 & 70 minutes.

The Lufthansa Airport Bus connects terminals 1 & 2 with Milan Central Station. They stop in Milan Fair and Fiera Milano City, as well as Pero/Rho by request. They run every 20 minutes.

There is 24-hour, free shuttle service from Terminal 1 to Terminal 2, leaving every 7-8 minutes.

Rail

The Malpensa Express train runs from the Terminal 1 & 2 rail stations to central Milan. They leave every half hour. In town, you can connect to the M1 & M2 Milan Metro lines. The trip takes about a half hour.

Taxis from the Airport to Milan

The taxi queues are in the Arrivals section on the ground floor of Terminal 1. The rate from Malpensa Airport to central Milan is $108 USD.

Milan Rental Cars

You can rent a car at Malpensa Airport or rent one online before you arrive at the airport. The Malpensa car rental desks are in the Arrivals Hall of Terminal 1. You can take the free shuttle bus to T1 from T2 if you land at T2.

The companies that rent cars at Malpensa Airport include Avis, Auto Europa, Dollar, Budget, Hertz, Europcar, Maggiore National, Locauto, Thrifty, Sixt and Goldcar.

Milan Cabs

Milan taxes are certainly not inexpensive, but this is the case in most areas of Italy. Hopping the metro or catching a bus is cheaper. If you need a ride later than midnight or 2AM when the buses and metro are no longer running, a taxi is your last, best option.

It's not easy to hail a taxi from the street, since they often will not stop. They are not supposed to stop at the curb on any street. You need to find a taxi rank or phone a cab.

The meter starts running when your cab comes to get you, if you call one. To catch one without booking by phone, the easiest places to catch cabs are at the central train station, Cadorna northern train station or Stazione Centrale. There are also small taxi ranks near Piazza del Duomo and Corso Buenas Aires.

Some unscrupulous drivers are always on the lookout for tourists, and they may try to charge more than the usual fare. Be sure they turn the meter on. The booking charge, if you call a cab to come to your location, pays for the time it takes to get there.

Most dispatchers and drivers do not speak English fluently, so you may want to learn a few major words before you arrive, or have your hotel concierge write down your destination for the driver.

Payment and Tipping for Taxi's

Typical fares for cabs (not counting driving to you if you book ahead):

- Taxi Start, sometimes called Normal Tariff: about $6 USD

- Taxi for each mile: about $2.11 USD

- Taxi for 1 hour of waiting: about $36 USD

You may tip your driver if you have a good, safe ride, but it is not common, nor expected. They will appreciate it if you do, though.

Public Transport in Milan

Milan's public transport system is efficient, and the preferred method of travel in and around the city.

The system includes:

- 70 surface lines that are run using buses, trams and trolleys

- Four subway/underground lines

- One suburban rail link, most of which is underground

The subway system runs from about 6AM until midnight each day. Some of the bus lines run during the night hours, as well. Buses and trams start at about 5AM and run until about 1AM. There are also several night lines for buses that run on Friday nights and Saturday nights.

Some of the tram lines still use vintage trams that were built back in the 1920s. In fact, Milan shipped 10 of these vehicles to San Francisco, where they are used as part of its streetcar line.

Passes & Tickets

You must buy a ticket before you board and it must be stamped properly in the small red machine at subway turnstiles and on trams or buses. Inspectors check the tickets and passes regularly, and if you have one that has not been properly activated, you will be assessed a large fine.

Tickets for urban transport are not as expensive as you might think. The standard transport tickets cost about $1.78 USD and they can be used within 90 minutes of their first stamping for transport via any surface mode, or one ride on the suburban train or subway.

A 24 hour pass is available for $5.35 USD and a 48-hour pass is $9.82 USD. These are a good way to go if you plan to use mainly mass transit during your stay. So, for a three-day stay, one 48-hour and one 24-hour pass will work well, unless you plan to use taxis. Children under the age of six ride for free.

You can purchase tickets and passes at multilingual vending machines found at subway stops, or from tobacco shops and newsstands. There is a ticket office at the main Duomo subway stop, as well.

4. Accommodations

There are many hotels of every class available in Milan. They have all the modern amenities you would expect. The hotels we have explored for you below have AT LEAST a "very good" rating from people who have stayed there.

Attractions in Italian Translated

Since many attractions are listed in Italian, and not logically extrapolated from the base words, we will translate those for you here:

- Teatro alla Scala – La Scala Opera House

- Corso Como – Design shop and restaurant

- Castello Sforzesco – Sforza Castle

- Boscoincitta – an urban park in Milan

- Metropoli – Commercial shopping center

- Monte Stella – Artificial hill and park

- Fiera Milano City – Exhibition and trade center

- Arco della Pace – Historic architectural building

- Chiesa di Sant Ambrogio – Church (Basilica) in Milan

- Pinacoteca di Brera – Art gallery - paintings

- Santa Maria Delle Grazie – Dominican convent & church

- Darsena – Milan harbor where canals meet

Prices for Luxury Hotels: $700 USD per night and up

TownHouse 33

- Close to Natural Science Museum, Sempione Park, Civic Museum of

Archeology, Castello Sforzesco, Corso Como, Pinacoteca di Brera, Teatro alla Scala, Piazza del Duomo, Galleria Vittorio Emanuele II, Cathedral of Milan

Italiana Hotels Milan Rho Fair

- Close to Arco della Pace, Milan Convention Center, Monte Stella, Metropoli, Boscoincitta, Arese Shopping Center, San Siro Stadium

UNA Hotel Malpensa

- Close to Arese Shopping Center, Teatro Sociale, Parco degli Aironi, Parco del Roccolo, Chiesa di Sant Ambrogio, Basilica di San Magno, Castle Park Legnano

Mandarin Oriental, Milan

- Close to Teatro alla Scala, Cathedral of Milan, Pinacoteca di Brera, Galleria Vittorio Emanuele II, Castello Sforzesco,

Piazza del Duomo, Sempione Park, Civic Museum of Archeology, Corso Como, Santa Maria delle Grazie

Bulgari Hotel Milan

- Close to Cathedral of Milan, Pinacoteca di Brera, Teatro alla Scala, Corso Como, Santa Maria Delle Grazie, Sempione Park, Civic Museum of Archeology, Piazza del Duomo, Castello Sforzesco, Galleria Vittorio Emanuele II

Park Hyatt Milano

- Close to Leonardo da Vinci Museum of Science and Technology, Piazza del Duomo, Cathedral of Milan, Santa Maria Delle Grazie, Sempione Park, Castello Sforzesco, Civic Museum of Archeology, Pinacoteca di Brera, Teatro alla Scala, Galleria Vittorio Emanuele II

Prices for Mid-Range Hotels: $ 200 USD to $500 USD per night

Marconi Hotel

- Close to Cathedral of Milan, Pinacoteca di Brera, Corso Como, Santa Maria delle Grazie, Civic Museum of Archeology, Arco della Pace, Piazza del Duomo, Sempione Park, Castello Sforzesco, Galleria Vittorio Emanuele II, Teatro alla Scala

The Square Milano Duomo

- Close to Piazza del Duomo, Cathedral of Milan, Teatro alla Scala, Galleria Vittorio Emanuele II, Santa Maria Delle Grazie, Leonadro da Vinci Museum of Science & Technology, Sempione Park, Pinacoteca di Brera, Castello Sforzesco, Civic Museum of Archeology

Palazzo Segreti

- Close to Piazza del Duomo, Museo Teatrale alla Scala, Piazza Cordusio, teatro Dal Verme, Piccolo Teatro Grassi

Room Mate Giulia

- Close to Piazza del Duomo, Cathedral of Milan, Leonardo da Vinci Museum of Science and Technology, Santa Maria delle Grazie, Sempione Park, Castello Sforzesco, Civic Museum of Archeology, Pinacoteca di Brera, Teatro alla Scala, Galleria Vittorio Emanuele II

Hotel Principe Di Savoia

- Close to Arco della Pace, Cathedral of Milan, Civic Museum of Archeology, Piazza del Duomo, Sempione Park, Castello Sforzesco, Galleria Vittorio Emanuele II, Pinacoteca di Brera, Teatro alla Scala, Corso Como

Senato Hotel Milano

- Close to Piazza del Duomo, Cathedral of Milan, Arco della Pace, Civic Museum of Archeology, Corso Como, Sempione Park, Castello Sforzesco, Galleria Vittorio Emanuele II, Pinacoteca di Brera, Teatro alla Scala

Prices for Cheapest Hotels: $100 USD per night and less

Hotel Studios

- Close to Corso Como, Castello Sforzesco, Pinacoteca di Brera, Galleria Vittorio Emanuele II, Teatro alla Scala, Cathedral of Milan, Monza Cathedral, Galleria Campari

Heart Milan Apartments - Duomo

- Close to Leonardo da Vinci Museum of Science and Technology, Cathedral of

Milan, Piazza del Duomo, Galleria Vittorio Emanuele II, Santa Maria Delle Grazie, Sempione Park, Pinacoteca di Brera, Castello Sforzesco, Teatro alla Scala, Civic Museum of Archeology

Grand Hotel Duca di Mantova

- Close to Civic Museum of Archeology, Cathedral of Milan, Sempione Park, Castello Sforzesco, Pinacoteca di Brera, Galleria Vittorio Emanuele II, Teatro alla Scala, Monza Cathedral, Galleria Campari, PalaSesto

AS Hotel dei Giovi

- Close to Autodromo Nazionale Monza, Church of St Francis of Assisi, Monza Park, Royal Villa of Monza, San Lorenzo Church, Monza Cathedral, PalaDesio

At Home - P.ta Venezia C.so Buenos Aires

- Close to Piazza del Duomo, Cathedral of Milan, Santa Maria Delle Grazie, Arco della Pace, Civic Museum of Archeology, Sempione Park, Castello Sforzesco, Galleria Vittorio Emanuele II, Pinacoteca di Brera, Teatro alla Scala, Corso Como

I Bravi

- Close to Cathedral of Milan, Metropoli, Pinacoteca di Brera, Teatro alla Scala, Sempione Park, Castello Sforzesco, Arco della Pace, Corso Como

Airbnb's

The average price for an Airbnb in Milan is $116 USD per night. This includes everything from single private rooms to large estates, suitable for groups.

Price range:

- $21 USD per night for a simple room with one bed and a shared bathroom

- $69 to $175 USD per night for a deluxe apartment with a private bathroom

- $350+ USD per night for a comfortable luxury condo with all the amenities

5. Sightseeing

Milan has much to offer sightseers, since it is a global hub of design and fashion. In addition to high end shops and restaurants, there are cathedrals, theaters, museums and many other buildings of archaeological interest, testifying to centuries of culture and art.

Il Duomo (Cathedral)

This is the Cathedral of Santa Maria Nascente. It holds about 40,000 people, making it one of the largest cathedrals in the world. It shows its Gothic style in a flamboyant way. Started in the 1300s, it would not be completed until early in the 1800s.

The cathedral roof has 135 delicately carved pinnacles of stone, and there are more than 2,000 statues on its exterior. The interior is starkly dim, with 52 giant pillars. Its stained-glass windows, most from the 1400s and 1500s, are the largest windows of this style in the world.

Leonardo da Vinci's Last Supper

The refectory of this Gothic church - Santa Maria delle Grazie – holds the priceless Last Supper by Leonardo da Vinci. The church and painting were damaged badly during WW II, and some old dome paintings were discovered while repair work was being done.

Most people visit the church to see the famous painting. It was originally painted in the 1400s. Rather than a static representation of the last meal of Christ and his apostles, da Vinci created a more dramatic scene. It began flaking off when the room's destruction left it open to rain and wind. It has already been painstakingly restored numerous times. This process will likely never be completely finished.

Castello Sforzesco

This red brick castle was constructed in 1368 and would be rebuilt in 1450. The current gate-tower is a 1900s reproduction of its original. Inside, you will find a group of museums featuring Italian art and sculpture. In the collection you will find Michelangelo's last art masterpiece, the Pietà Rondanini. Other museums in the castle feature medieval weapons and armor, a musical history collection, Egyptian and prehistoric antiquities and decorative art.

Sant'Ambrogio

Saint Ambrose founded this church in 386 AD. He is the patron saint of Milan. Today, the church is still a Romanesque architectural masterpiece, built in the 1100s around an earlier, 800s church. There are many things to see in this church. They include an atrium that has carved stone capitals and portals. On the church's right side, past the last chapel, you can see a mosaic dome built in the 300s.

Galleria Vittorio Emanuele II

This large area forms one side of Piazza del Duomo and opens on its other side on Piazza della Scala. It was built in the 1800s, and was, in its time, the largest of Europe's shopping arcades.

This galleria stands as a testament to modern Italian architecture, with its glass and iron construction. It is still a vibrant, beautiful place there the locals meet for coffee or lunch in one of its cafes, or shop in the luxury stores. It is an integral part of life in Milan, and is often referred to as simply "il salotto", which means "the salon".

6. Eat & Drink

Milan has a regional Italian cuisine, which uses rice more than pasta, and does not feature tomatoes as much as they are used in other areas. It includes dishes like "cotoletta alla milanese", which is breaded veal, turkey or pork.

Some of the more popular Milanese dishes include ossobuco, which is a stewed veal shank in sauce, and cassoeula, which is made from pork rib chops with Savoy cabbage and sausage. They are also often fond of Brasato, a stewed pork or beef with potatoes and wine and busecca, a stewed tripe served with beans.

Fine Dining Restaurants

Sadler – approximately $300 USD for two

The chef describes the food here as evolutionary, yet modern. They specialize in Mediterranean dishes, seafood and Italian dishes. They pay special attention to traditional ways of cooking, and take pride in the way their dishes are presented.

Among the favorite dishes at Sadler is risotto with tuna bottarga and lime. The shaved bottarga is delicate and delicious. They also serve wonderful pasta with seafood.

Iyo – approximately $180 USD for two

Iyo specializes in Sushi, Seafood and Fusion dishes. They have a competent and friendly staff, and reasonable prices, considering the fine dining tag. People enjoy their edamame, dumplings, rolls and sashimi. They have a wonderful wine selection, too.

The favorite dishes here include shrimp fried rice and shrimp tempura, in portions enough to fill you up before dessert. Their hibachi fried rice gets rave reviews, as does the sashimi sampler, with its lovely presentation.

Alice – approximately $240 USD for two

Alice specializes in Mediterranean, seafood and Italian dishes. The food is a mix of tradition and innovation, done in a smooth manner. The quality and freshness of their ingredients are amazing.

You might like to try their three types of amuse bouche, their fried octopus, tartare of the day, and their "Around Campari" dessert.

Midrange Restaurants

La Dogana del Buongusto – approximately $84 for two

Serving European, Mediterranean and Italian food, this popular restaurant is a winner with their diners. The staff are very attentive and the sommelier can recommend the perfect wine to compliment your meal.

Among their favorite dishes are the veal cutlet (in a huge size) and their smoked fish. The skewered meat is also very popular.

TOM. – approximately $84 USD for two

TOM specializes in International, European and Italian cuisine. They have polite waiters and quick service. The ambiance is fairly laid back, so you can get comfortable quite easily. You might like to try their tartare of tuna, the Baccala with almonds, or their quinoa salad with warm roasted vegetables.

Albufera – approximately $72 USD for two

Albufera has been recommended in city restaurant listings, and you won't be disappointed. Among their most popular dishes are their mini hamburger, octopus and tortilla. From the croquettes to the picanha and gambas to their paella, the food is delicious. Try to save room for their apple pie for dessert.

Cheap Eats

Do You Fusion? - approximately $24 USD for two

Specializing in Sushi, American and Japanese food and the fusion of them together, this is a popular place for inexpensive and creative meals. You'll feel right at home, with their friendly and helpful staff. It's a wonderful place for a quiet or romantic meal.

What to eat here? There are so many favorites, including uramaki BBQ, salmon, and baked avocado with cheeses and peanuts.

Panini Durini – approximately $36 USD for two

This restaurant is typically crowded because the food is so tasty, but the staff members are quite friendly and the service is still fast. Some of the favorite dishes at Panini Durini include insalate crocante with bacon, potato wedges and zucchini grigliate.

Vinh Ha Long – approximately $36 USD for two

You can discover authentic Vietnamese cuisine at Vinh Ha Long. The dishes are light and easily digested, compared to many of Milan Chinatown's Asian offerings. Appetizing starters include fried rolls and rolls with leafy pork and shrimp. For the main course, you may want to try the Pho: Noodles with herbs and beef broth. Some of the other favorites here include squid stuffed with tender pork with long-boiled sweet sauce, or the seafood with lime and chili.

7. Culture and Entertainment

Rome is representative of "old" Italy, and Milan represents "new" Italy. It is the most modern Italian city, yet it still maintains its past history well.

When you first see Milan, it seems like a stylish and bustling city, with its elegant shops and display windows. It still has many buildings that are architecturally significant. It just takes a bit more exploring to find them than in cities like Rome.

Spending even a few days here can give you a better idea of Milan's culture. From the chic appeal of the Brera district to the churches and other historic buildings, you will discover that Milan has history in every corner. It is also rich with history in fashion, art, sport, literature and theater.

Opera at Teatro alla Scala

This is considered by many people to be the most prestigious of all the world's opera houses. It has been home for many operatic singers and composers. The audience is thought to be the most demanding of opera audiences in Italy. It's difficult to get tickets, but you can check with your hotel concierge. When there are no rehearsals going on, you may be able to get in to see the interior, which is truly grand.

Pinacoteca di Brera

The Palazzo di Brera was built in the 1600s and 1700s. It started as a Jesuit college, but has been a fine arts academy since 1776. It contains an art museum, observatory and library. A good portion of their art was added to the museum as Italian churches were demolished or closed. There are many paintings by masters of art from northern Italy.

Poldi-Pezzoli Museum

This art museum is in an elegant patrician house. The artists represented include Mantegna, Guardi, Botticelli and others. They also house weapons, armor, pottery, porcelains, bronzes, silver and jewelry. There are also showcased textiles, including hand-worked lace, tapestries and Persian and Flemish carpets.

Piazza dei Mercanti

Milan has many high-rise buildings, so, unlike cities like Rome, it's harder to find areas that show medieval Milan. But just five minutes from Piazza del Duomo is a tiny street, Piazza dei Mercanti, and it's like walking backward in time to the Middle Ages. On one side is the 1233 town hall, Palazzo della Ragione.

The location of the town hall made this area the heart of politics in Milan, and the stone arcade created a commercial square, too. The other side is

1316 Loggie degli Osii, with its black & white marble, which originally housed notary and judicial offices.

Milan Night-Life

After the cocktail hour has ended, some lounges become formal dining restaurants. When dinner time has passed, some turn into nightclubs. The late night scene starts at 10:30 pm or so, and runs through 4 am, with many types of clubs to enjoy.

Alcatraz

This is certainly not anything like California's Alcatraz. It is a large venue, hosting many types of events. Within 3000 square feet of modern and elegant décor, you'll find lots of tourists and locals partying the night away. Alcatraz hosts DJ events, live music and even fashion shows and TV shoots, so there is always something going on.

Blue Note

The Blue Note Jazz Club originated in New York, but the Milan location has a different feel, even though the sound is like the original. They have live music every night of the week. Many fans from Milan come out for the blues and jazz, and tourists love it, too.

H Club>Diana

This club is most alive during the summer, when they use the garden area. When colder weather arrives, visitors will notice that the interior is actually striking, too. This is much more than a bar in a hotel – it's quite hip and trendy.

8. Special Events in Milan

Corteo dei Re Magi   **January 6**

This is a religious festival, celebrating the feast of the Epiphany, that day when the three wise men visited the stable where Jesus was born. In the Milan celebration, three volunteers act as those wise men, and lead a parade in town.

Milan Fashion Week   **February &**
September (held two times each year)

First held in 1958, Milan Fashion Week is one of four large, important fashion shows in the world. It is held two times each year, in February and September. It's a trade show for high-fashion clothing. The other cities are Paris, London and New York City.

Carnival Ambrosiano — March/April

This carnival is all about happiness and partying. It starts on the first Saturday in the Lenten calendar. The date will vary, and depends on when Easter Sunday is for Catholics in a given year.

Del Naviglio — June

Live music and parades mark Del Naviglio. There are also various other entertainment events, and vendors line the canals with goods for sale.

Festival Latino Americano — June

The people of Milan let their hair down for this lively festival, and celebrate Latino food, culture and music.

The Italian Grand Prix — September

This sporting event is held annually, and attracts large local and international crowds. It is held early in September, and the city is quite busy during this time. If you're into racing, it's a great time to visit. If you're not, you might want to check the dates and book your trip during a different week, for better hotel rates and smaller crowds.

The Milano Film Festival   September

This is almost as important in Milan as Fashion Week. Tourists and locals enjoy a full week of short films that were directed by locals. It's a very popular time of year in Milan.

The Milan Jazz Festival   November-December

The jazz festival of Milan attracts lovers of jazz from countries near and far. The jazz clubs in Milan are quite famous. The festival lasts a month.

9. Safety in Milan

The capital of fashion in Europe is also the financial and economic center of Italy. The center of town is quite safe, even for women that are travelling alone. However, there are areas where pickpockets frequent.

To minimize the chance of being targeted by pickpockets:

- Keep your wallet in a front pocket.

- Don't carry extra cash you don't need.

- Carry a shoulder bag or a concealed money pouch instead of a backpack.

- Be wary of people acting strangely or trying to divert your attention, as they may be trying to pick your pocket, especially if they are in small groups.

- Don't wear flashy, expensive jewelry.

- Don't leave your cell phone on a table at restaurants or cafes.

- Pay attention when you are using an ATM.

- If someone tries to grab your bag, let it go. Don't risk violence. Milan is not a haven for violent criminals, but it's best to be safe.

- Be especially vigilant for pickpockets at tourist areas like subways, airports, train stations, beaches, hotels, restaurants, monuments and museums.

10. Conclusion

We hope our travel guide has helped you in planning a memorable and enjoyable trip to Milan. We've shown you well-known sights and pointed out a few lesser known ones, too.

Your itinerary for Milan now may include:

- Your choice for the best hotel

- A list of sights we have helped you to hand pick

- Some good dining options

- Tips on money and tipping

- How to best get around town

If this will be your first visit to Milan, we've pointed out the "must see" places, but enough off the tourist track that you can get a feel for the city, too.

We've helped you in this guide to take some of the effort out of planning your trip, which leaves you free to take in the sights.

Made in United States
North Haven, CT
21 March 2025